Tiny Paws and Big Black Eyes

Whose little baby are you?

A Baby in a Den

bamboo forest

There is a **cave** in a **bamboo** forest.

den

In the cave is a **den**.

by Ellen Lawrence

Educational Consultant:
Dee Reid

...s for Reading with Your Child

- Set aside at least 10 to 15 minutes each day for reading.

- Find a quiet place to sit with no distractions. Turn off the TV, music and screens.

- Encourage your child to hold the book and turn the pages.

- Before reading begins, look at the pictures together and talk about what you see.

- If the reader gets stuck on a word, try reading to the end of the sentence. Often by reading the word in context, he or she will be able to figure out the unknown word. Looking at the pictures can help, too.

- Words shown in **bold** are explained in the glossary on pages 22–23.

Above all enjoy the time together and make reading fun!

Book Band Blue

Download a panda factfile:
www.rubytuesdaybooks.com/factfiles

The den is the home of a tiny baby.

Who does this little baby belong to?

mother giant
panda

two-day-old
panda cub

The tiny baby is a **panda** cub.

It belongs to a giant panda.

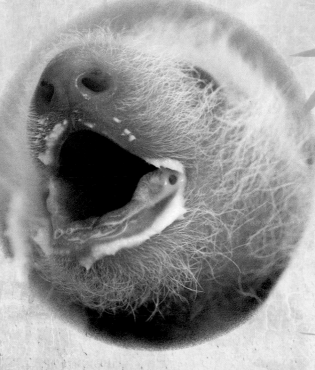

The panda cub drinks milk
from her mother.

Every day the panda cub grows bigger.

When the panda cub is two weeks old, she has black legs, black ears and black eye patches.

two-week-old cub

The mother panda keeps the cub warm with her big, furry body.

four-week-old cub

Soon the cub has thick fur and her eyes have opened.

When the mother panda goes to find food, the cub waits in the den.

The mother panda licks the
cub to keep her clean.

When the cub is four months old, she plays with her mum outside the den.

When playtime is over, the cub has a drink of milk.

Pandas are very good at climbing trees.

When the cub is five months old, she climbs…

...and climbs...

...and climbs.

Pandas like to eat bamboo.

mother panda

bamboo

When the panda cub is about six months old, she tries eating bamboo.

six-month-old cub

It is very tough and crunchy.

When the panda cub
is two years old, she is
ready to leave her mum.

Now, she lives alone in
the bamboo forest.

When she is about
six years old,
she will be ready
to have a cub
of her own.

Glossary

bamboo
A kind of grass plant. Bamboo has thick, tough stems that are hollow like a tube.

cave
A room-like space that has formed in rock. A cave might form in a cliff or a hillside.

den

An animal's home. A den might be inside a cave or tree stump. It might also be underground.

panda

A kind of bear with black and white fur. Pandas come from China.

Panda Quiz

1. What colour is a panda's fur?

2. Where did the panda cub live?

3. In what ways does the mother panda take care of her cub?

4. What do pandas eat?

5. What is happening in the pictures on page 14 and 15?